Craven-Pamlico-Carteret
Regional Library

D1275396

Science Fun

Hands-on science with **DR. ZED**

Owl Books are published by Greey de Pencier Books Inc.,
179 John Street, Suite 500, Toronto, Ontario M5T 3G5

The Owl colophon is a trademark of Owl Children's Trust Inc.
Greey de Pencier Books Inc. is a licensed user of trademarks of Owl Children's Trust Inc.

Text and illustrations © 1998 Owl Books. This book contains material that previously
appeared in *Dr. Zed's Science Surprises* © 1989 Greey de Pencier Books,
More Science Surprises from Dr. Zed © 1992 Greey de Pencier Books, and *Chickadee* Magazine.

All rights reserved. No part of this book may be reproduced or copied in any form
without written consent from the publisher.

Distributed in the United States by Firefly Books (U.S.) Inc.,
230 Fifth Avenue, Suite 1607, New York, NY 10001.

Dedication

To my wife Marion for her constant support; to our family: Lynda, Donna and Ted, Sandra and Bill;
to our grandchildren: Haley, Rory, Taylor Rose and Jamie Lynn; to my friend Erle; to the editors
of *Chickadee* for their interest and suggestions; to the children who show me the joy to be found
in experimenting with everyday things – it is with them that I share one-half of the profits from
this book through charitable organizations that care for children around the world.

The publishers acknowledge the generous support of the Canada Council for the Arts and the
Ontario Arts Council for our publishing program. We would like to acknowledge the work of
Lizann Flatt, Janis Nostbakken and Marilyn Baillie (editors) on *Science Fun*.

Cataloguing in Publication Data

Penrose, Gordon, 1925–
Science fun : hands-on science with Dr. Zed

Includes index.
ISBN 1-895688-73-6 (bound) ISBN 1-895688-74-4 (pbk.)

1. Science - Experiments - Juvenile literature. I. Title.

Q164.P468 1998   j507'.8   C97-932198-0

Photography: Ray Boudreau and Tony Thomas (page 23)
Illustrations: Tina Holdcroft and Andrew Plewes (pages 18–19)
Cover Design: Gary Beelik

Design & Art Direction: Wycliffe Smith, Julia Naimska, Gary Beelik

The activities in this book have been tested and are safe when conducted as instructed.
The author and publisher accept no responsibility for any damage caused or sustained by the
use or misuse of ideas or material featured in the activities in *Science Fun*.

Printed in Hong Kong

A B C D E F G

Science Fun

Hands-on science with **DR. ZED**

Gordon Penrose

compiled and edited by Lizann Flatt

Owl

Craven-Pamlico-Carteret
Regional Library

Contents

Introduction 6

Your Body 8
   Fingerprints 10
   Finger Power 12
   Taste Test 14
   Color Vision 16
   Eye Openers 18
   Hole in Your Hand 20
   Body Tricks 22

Nature All Around 24
   Plant Power 26
   Plant Fun 28
   Night Lights 30
   Water Power 32
   Spin Away! 34
   Bubble, Bubble 36

Always the Same 38
   Water Surprises 40
   Lost and Found 42

Bag Boggle 44

High and Dry 46

Heart to Heart 48

Up and Away! 50

Paper Power 52

Card Trick 54

Change 56

Bathtub Boats 58

Elec-tricks 60

Secret Messages 62

Presto! Change-o! 64

Egg Games 66

Egg-citing Eggs 68

Hot and Cold 70

What Happened! 72

Science Concepts 78

Index 80

Introduction

The activities in this book have been carefully selected to give children a hands-on introduction to science. In doing these simple experiments, children can make a variety of discoveries that will surprise and delight them. Above all, it is hoped that these activities will encourage children to explore and experiment further to discover for themselves the many surprises science holds.

There are no wrong outcomes to the activities — every finding is valid and bound to stimulate lots of questions. The *What Happened!* section at the end of the book suggests explanations and insights into those science concepts that can be discussed simply with children ages 4 to 8. These notes also include the answers to the special challenges scattered throughout the book. The *Science Concepts* section lists scientific principles and points to the experiments that explore those principles: some of these concepts are not discussed in the *What Happened!* section because they are too abstract for young children. An adult or older child will find this listing of scientific concepts useful. The final section of the book is an index to help locate individual experiments.

Meet Dr. Zed

Gordon Penrose is the man behind Dr. Zed. A retired Master Teacher of science, Gordon now travels extensively, giving workshops on his experiments for children and educators. He has made more than 4,000 presentations and developed more than 385 experiments so far. Gordon maintains that interaction with children and their teachers is a constant inspiration to him. Over the years, his contributions to science and children's education have been gratefully acknowledged by many organizations. He has been made a Fellow of the Ontario Institute for Studies in Education, has received the Michael Smith Award for science promotion with children and teachers, and he has been named a Member of the Order of Canada.

Your Body

What was that noise? What's that smell? Your body gives you answers to questions every day. Your five senses let you see, hear, smell, touch and taste things to learn more about them. Each sense uses a body part to do most of the sensing. You see with your eyes, you smell with your nose, you taste with your tongue, you hear with your ears and you touch with your skin.

Find out more about how your senses work. Sounds are made when air moves quickly back and forth. The air reaches your ears, which send messages to your brain to tell you what you're hearing. You can help your ears catch more air vibrations. Cup your hands just behind your ears while listening to something in front of you. That sounds better! Did you know your sense of touch isn't the same all over your body? Without touching your skin, lightly brush your finger across the hairs on your forearm.

Your fingertip can barely feel the hair, but the skin on your arm feels the movement. Sense-ational!

Fingerprints

**True or false? All members of
your family have the same fingerprints.
Find the answer by collecting and
comparing the fingerprints of your
family and friends. Be sure to wash
your hands before and after
following these steps.**

1. Lightly rub a thin coating of lipstick onto your fingertip.

2. Carefully place your smudged finger on a piece of clear sticky tape.

3. Peel the tape off your finger and stick it onto a piece of clean paper.

WHICH FINGERPRINT TYPE IS THE MOST COMMON?

**Once you've collected prints of
a number of people, compare
them to each other and to
these fingerprint types.**

Are you a loop, a whorl or an arch?

Arch

Loop

Whorl

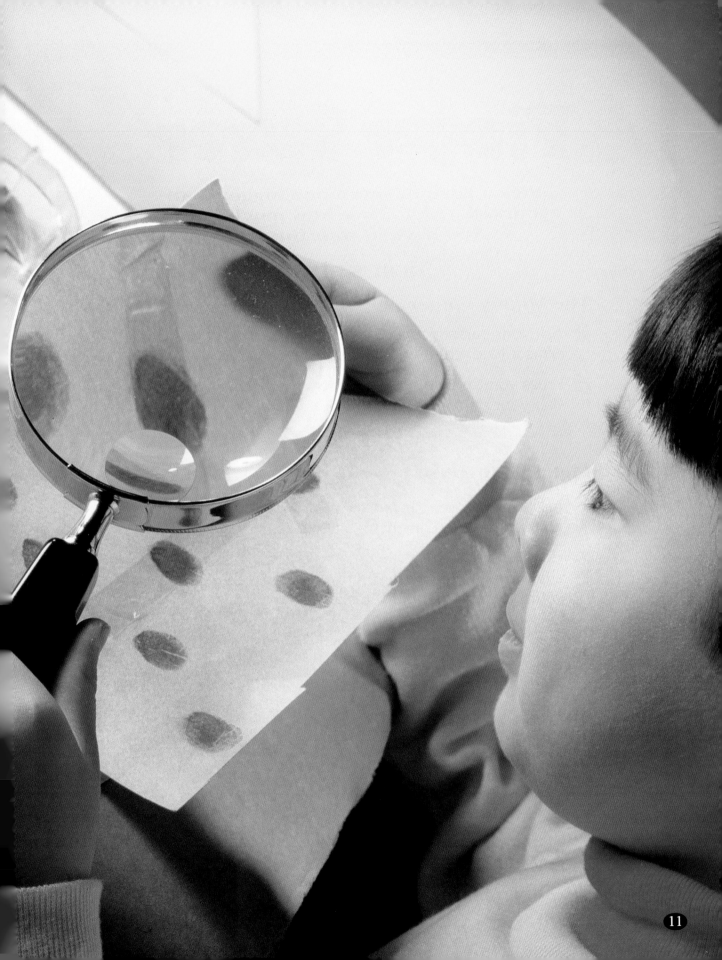

Finger Power

Pick a partner (even one bigger than yourself!) and prove how much power you have in your fingers.

HERE'S HOW:

The Mighty Finger

1. Ask your partner to sit in a straight-backed chair with arms folded, chin up, head high.

2. Press your index finger against your partner's forehead. Can your partner get up out of the chair?

Fighting Fingers

1. Ask your partner to stand with arms fully outstretched and fists pressed firmly together, one on top of the other.

2. Hold out your index fingers and quickly strike them sideways, in opposite directions, against the fists. Can your partner still hold the fists together?

NOW TEST YOUR FINGER POWER AGAINST A PENNY.

Put your knuckles together. Ask your partner to help you raise your ring fingers and place a penny between them. Here's the challenge: can you drop the penny?

Be a penny pincher!

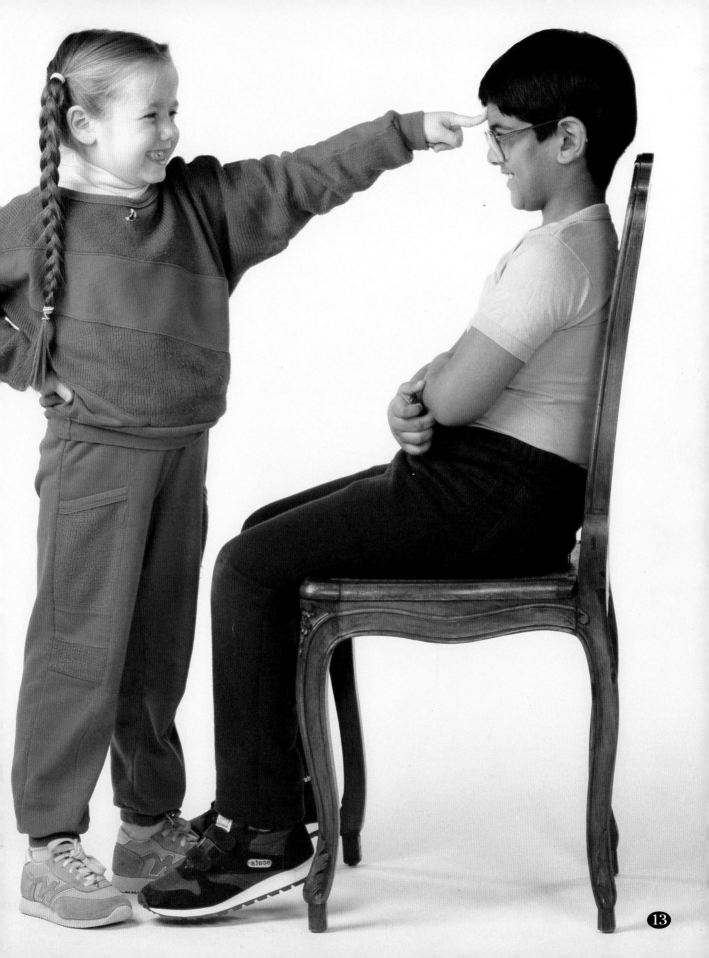

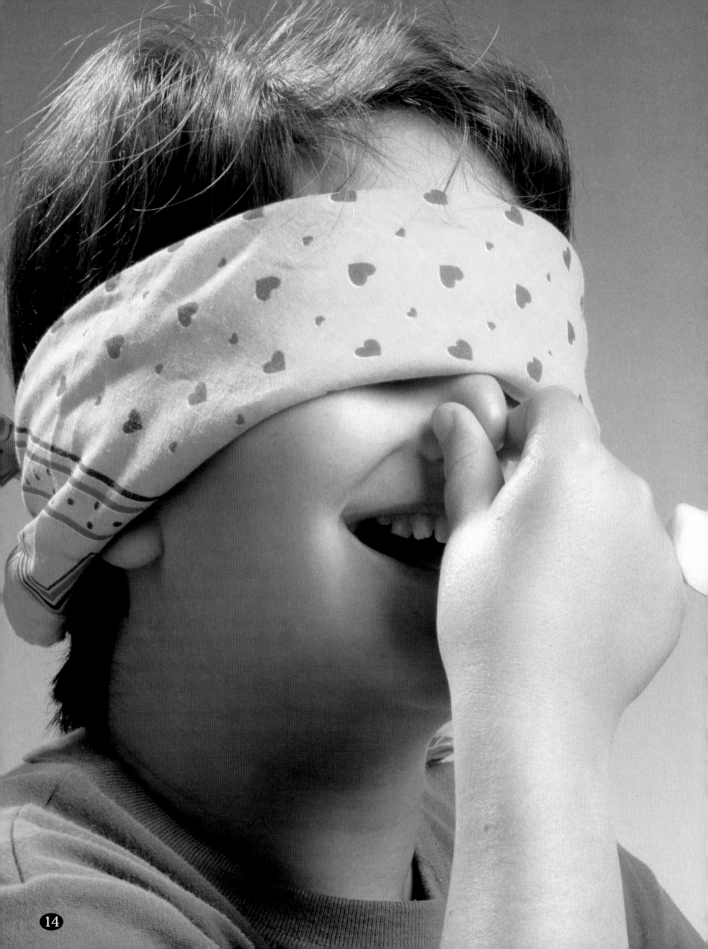

Taste Test

Which would you rather eat, a raw potato or a raw apple? Take a taste test to find out.

HERE'S HOW:

1. Start with peeled slices of uncooked potato and apple.

2. Cover your eyes with a blindfold.

3. Tightly hold your nose with one hand.

4. Take a bite of each slice.
   Can you tell which is which?

TRY THE SAME TEST WITH FRUIT JUICE.

Hold your nose and take a sip of grape juice, then of apple juice. Can you tell them apart?

The nose knows!

Color Vision

How much do you know about colors?
Is black ink really black?

1. Draw a heavy black dot with a water-soluble marker on a paper towel or coffee filter.

2. Now put a drop of water directly on top of the dot.

3. Watch the dot come apart. What colors do you see?

Three colors...or more?

1. Mix a drop each of red, yellow and blue food coloring in a small amount of water.

2. Fold a coffee filter in half and then into quarters. Place the narrow end in the mixture.

3. Let the filter soak up the mixture, then open it up. So many colors!

Try bubbling a second color over the first.

SPATTER PATTERNS

Mix a small spoonful of detergent, a large spoonful of water and eight drops of food coloring in a small glass. Now hold the glass over some paper and blow into the mixture with a straw. Move the glass around as the bubbles spill onto the paper. What spatter patterns!

MARKER

Eye Openers

**Can you really believe what you see?
Look carefully at each of these
pictures to find out.**

1 How many faces do you see?

2 Which flower center
is the smallest?

3 How many animals
can you find here?

4 Stare at
the black
squares
and count
to ten.
What else
do you
see?

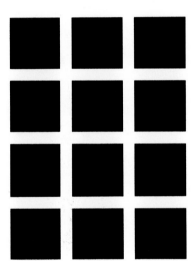

5 Are these stars
the same color?

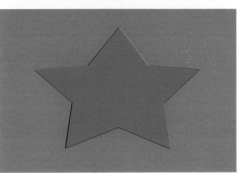

Wow!
A
floating
finger!

**MAKE YOUR OWN
OPTICAL ILLUSION.**

Hold your index fingers slightly apart
in front of your eyes. Stare at an object
beyond your fingers. What do you see
floating between your fingers?

Hole in Your Hand

**Do you have X-ray vision?
Follow these steps to see a hole
right through your hand!**

1. Roll a piece of paper about 30 cm (12 in) long into a tube or use an empty paper towel roll.

2. Look straight ahead at some object or spot on the wall.

3. Hold the tube up to one eye so that it completely covers the eye.

4. Hold your other hand, palm open and facing you, half-way along the tube.

5. Keep looking at the object with both eyes.

DID YOU KNOW YOU CAN PUSH A QUARTER THROUGH A HOLE THE SIZE OF A DIME?

Cut a dime-size hole in the center of a piece of paper. Fold the paper in half. Then place the coin in the center of the fold. Hold the outer edges of the fold, pull upward and wiggle the paper back and forth to ease the quarter through the hole.

Does this make CENTS?

Body Tricks

Surprise yourself with these body tricks.

HERE'S HOW:

Hop Stopper

1 Bend over and grab your toes.

2 Keep your knees slightly bent.

3 Try to hop forward. Can you hop backward?

Balancing Act

1 Balance on one foot and count to ten.

2 Have a rest.

3 Balance on one foot again, this time with your eyes closed. What number can you count to before you fall over?

Fool your friends!

QUICK! WHICH IS BIGGER, YOUR FOOT OR YOUR FOREARM?

Find out for sure by measuring your foot from heel to toe with a ruler or measuring tape. Then measure your arm from wrist to elbow. Were you right?

Nature All

Have you ever planted a seed, watched a rain storm, or eaten something? You've done at least one of these things. When you plant seeds you're helping nature. If you watch a rain storm you're seeing nature in action. Everything we eat comes from nature. We live with nature all around us, and we are part of nature.

Nature is made up of things like plants, animals, people, forests, mountains, deserts, oceans, lakes, rivers and weather – just about everything on the planet.

Find out more about nature right where you live. Watch a tree or a plant or a patch of grass for a bit. Do the leaves have bites out of them? Do you see any insects there? Are they eating the plant or other insects? If you find a spider web, can you see the spider? If you watch long enough, can you see it catch a fly? Watch your pet dog or cat. What does it do when you let it outside? Does it sniff out other animals? That's nature in action.

Plant Power

Grow some light-seeking, hole-peeking beans.

HERE'S HOW:

1. Cut a circle the size of a small juice can in one end of a shoe box.

2. Plant two dried navy or kidney beans in a small plastic container filled with soil.

3. Stand the container in the end of the box opposite the hole.

4. Put the lid on the box and set it in a sunny place. Check it every day and water the beans every few days.

5. When your plant begins to peek through the hole, take off the lid to see how it grew. We've snipped away the side of the box to show you what happened.

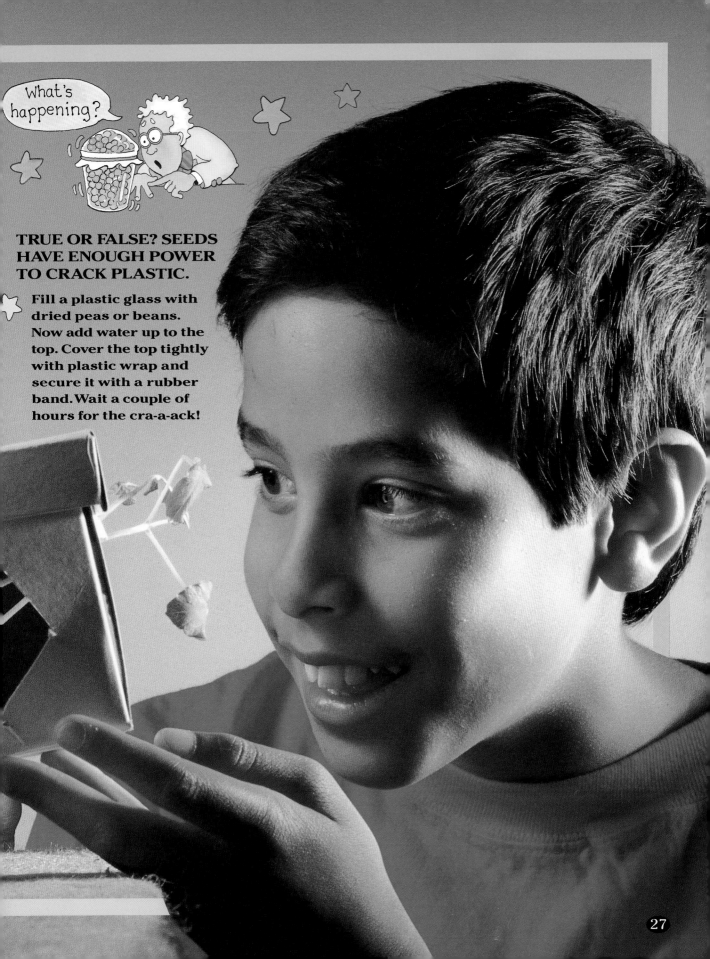

What's happening?

TRUE OR FALSE? SEEDS HAVE ENOUGH POWER TO CRACK PLASTIC.

Fill a plastic glass with dried peas or beans. Now add water up to the top. Cover the top tightly with plastic wrap and secure it with a rubber band. Wait a couple of hours for the cra-a-ack!

Plant Fun

**Here are some absorbing tricks
to try with veggies.**

Celery Slurp

1. Fill a tall glass with water and mix in about 20 drops of food coloring (not green).

2. Using a stalk of celery with the wide end cut off, set the middle, leafy part in the water with the cut end down.

3. After about a day in the colored water, your greens won't be green. What a change! Does the same thing happen if you try it with a flower?

This one will grow on you. It's tops!

SPROUT A CARROT TOP

Cut off the top of a carrot. Set the carrot top cut side down in a saucer of water, and put the saucer in a sunny window. Watch it for a week, making sure you refill the water when it gets low. What happened to the carrot top?

Night Lights

**Have you ever wondered if the
moon changes in size? Follow these steps to
see if it really does.**

1. Watch for a full moon. When it first rises, the moon often looks very large. Look at it through a hole in three-ring-binder paper.

2. Later, when the moon is high in the sky and appears to be smaller, look at it again through the same hole. It's the same as before!

> How do you do?
> I do like dew!

MAKE DEW

On a hot day, fill a glass with cold water and ice. Put the glass in the sunshine or where it will be warm. In a few minutes, your glass should be dewy on the outside. Where did that water come from?

Water Power

Where's the beach?
Make waves with this ocean in a jar.

1. Put about ten drops of food coloring into a large empty jar. Pour in water until the jar is half full.

2. Fill the rest of the jar with vegetable oil. Screw the lid on tightly.

3. Hold the jar on its side and slowly rock it back and forth. Look at those waves!

THE THIRSTY PINECONE

Find a dried pinecone that has fallen off a tree. Put the dried cone into a glass of hot tap water. In about five minues, what happens to the cone?

Hmmm, how absorbing.

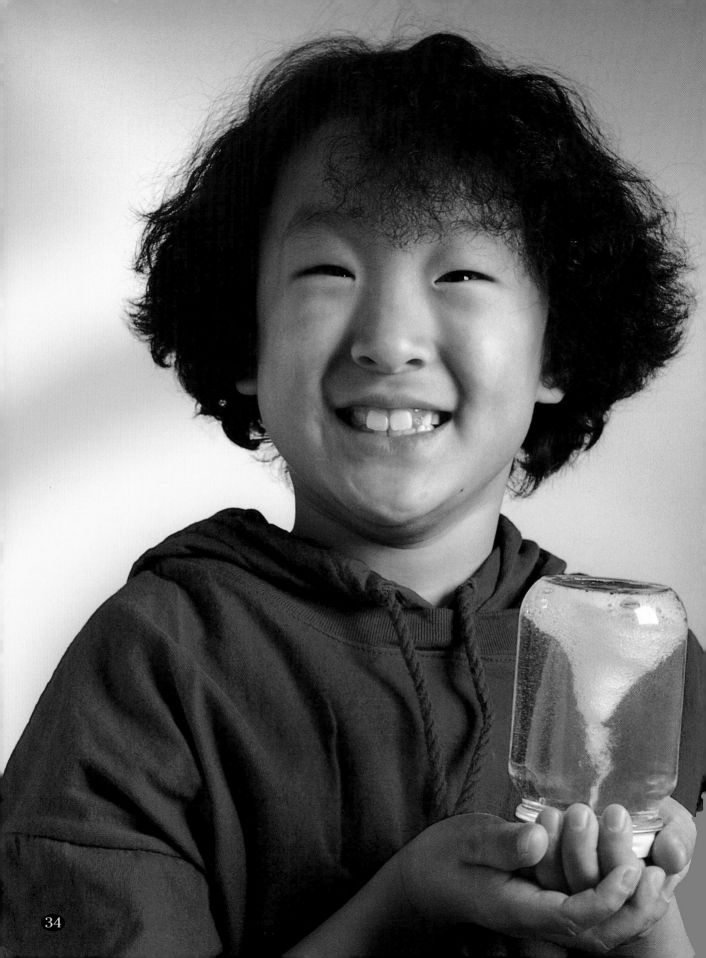

Spin Away!

Spin a Tornado

1. Fill a small jar with water.

2. Dab your finger into a bit of liquid soap, then dip your finger into the water in the jar.

3. Screw the lid on the jar tightly. Hold the jar upside down in the palm of your hand.

4. Swirl the jar in small, tight circles. Wow! The tornado appears like magic!

SPIN A TREAT

Leave a small carton of whipping cream out of the refrigerator for a few hours. Pour it into a clean plastic jar or container. Add five clean marbles and screw on the lid. Now shake and twist the jar for five to ten minutes until the cream changes to a runny liquid and a soft paste. Spread the soft stuff on your toast. Psst . . . it's butter!

Share the shaking with a friend if you get tired.

Bubble, Bubble

Soda water can make your food do some funny things!

Dancing Raisins

1. Fill a glass with soda water.
2. Drop a few raisins into the glass. Wow! Watch them dance.

Swimming Spaghetti

1. Fill a glass with soda water and add a little blue food coloring.
2. Now drop in some pieces of dry uncooked spaghetti. Up they swim and down they dive into the deep blue sea.

DO YOU KNOW WHAT RAISINS USED TO BE?

Leave your raisins in soda water overnight. Take a look at them the next morning and see what you find.

Always the

Have you ever asked a question and been told that it's just the way things are? You might not like an answer like that, but some things really are always the same. You can count on them to be that way. A mirror always shows you what you look like. A book will always stay on the table until something makes it move – maybe when you pick it up to read it. You can blow up a balloon because air always takes up space. If it's made right, a paper glider will always fly through the air for a bit. Things that are always the same are like rules that can't be broken.

Here's something you can always count on. Slowly pour some thick syrup onto a plate. See how it piles up before spreading out? That happens because the syrup is thick. If you pour water onto a plate, it just spreads out. The water doesn't have the same property of thickness as the syrup. Honey and molasses work like syrup too. Give it a try!

Same

Water Surprises

**Play the master magician and perform the
magic arrow flip trick.**

HERE'S HOW:

1. Draw a big arrow on an index card.
2. Hold the card upright a hand's length behind an empty glass. Look at the arrow.
3. Fill the glass with water. PRESTO! The arrow points the other way!

It must be magic!

THE DISAPPEARING STRAW

Fill a plastic glass with water. Put a
straw in the water and look at it
through the side of the glass. Move
the straw slowly around the inside
of the glass. Wow! Two straws! Move
it some more. Now no bottom straw.
Keep moving the straw around to
find it again...all in one piece.

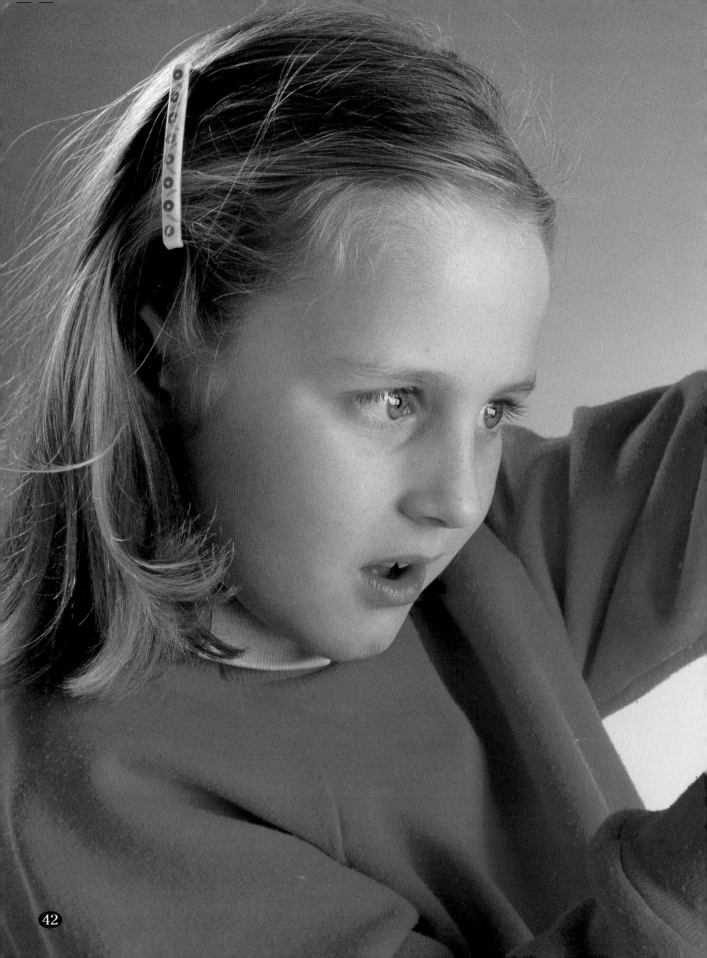

Lost and Found

Make a coin disappear right before your very eyes!

HERE'S HOW:

1. Fill a glass with water.

2. Put a coin in the palm of your hand.

3. Place the glass on top of the coin and look down through it to see the coin.

4. Now put your other hand on top of the glass and look for the coin through the side of the glass. Is it still there?

TRY THIS PENCIL TRICK!

Stick a pencil in a glass of water and look at it through the side of the glass. What happens to the pencil?

How did it break?

Bag Boggle

Wow! It's the no-leak lunch bag trick!

1. Fill a plastic sandwich bag with water and knot it.

2. Hold the bag over a sink with one hand.

3. Push a pencil through one side of the bag and out the other. Ta-da! No leaks.

   See how many more pencils you can push through.

NO-BUDGE LUNCH BAG

Open up a plastic sandwich bag inside a glass and push it tightly against the bottom and sides. Next, bring the top of the bag up and over the rim of the glass and secure it with a rubber band. Reach to the bottom and try to pull the bag out of the glass. It's there to stay!

It's really stuck!

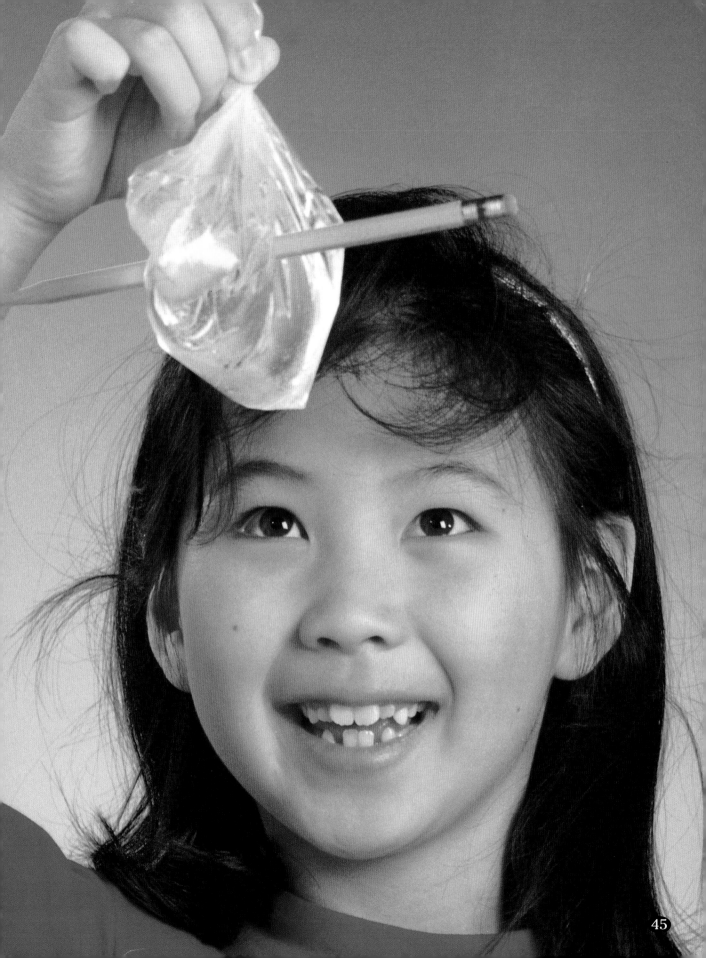

High and Dry

What goes under water but never gets wet? Follow these steps to find the answer.

1 Fill a sink or basin with water.

2 Pack some tissue into the bottom of a drinking glass so that it stays in place when the glass is turned upside down.

3 Hold the glass upside down and push it straight into the water without tipping it.

4 Pull the glass straight up out of the water. Now pull out the tissue. Is it wet or dry? What happens when you tip the glass?

HOW MANY TIMES CAN YOU FOLD A PIECE OF PAPER IN HALF? TWENTY, THIRTY, FORTY TIMES?

Guess again and then try folding paper yourself to see if you are right. Use any kind of paper, from tissue to cardboard.

...5...6 ...7...8 ...?!

Heart to Heart

**Roses are red, violets are blue,
Hugs and twirls, from me to you.**

Hugging Hearts

1. Trace the heart pattern at left onto a piece of paper.

2. Cut out the traced pattern, fold it over the middle of a pencil and tape it in place.

3. Can you make the hearts hug by blowing in between them?

WHIRLING TWIRLER

Fold an index card in half. Draw a large red heart on one side and a smiling face on the other. Now put the folded card on the end of a pencil. To hold the card in place, staple it together on both sides of the pencil. Gently hold the pencil between your palms and rub them together.

Up and Away!

It's a bird! It's a plane! No, it's a soaring straw!

1. Tape a paper clip to one end of a straw.

2. Cut two strips from the short side of a piece of notebook paper.

3. Tape the strips into loops. Then tape one loop to each end of the straw. (See picture.)

4. Hold the plane with the paper clip end forward and the loops up, and launch it. The plane flies!

Make Zoomers with your friends and see whose sails the farthest!

ZOOMERS

Cut a big straw in half. Tape one end of one piece closed. Now slide this half over the end of a thinner straw. Blow through the thin straw. Zoom! The big straw is off and away.

Paper Power

Which of these paper shapes will hold up a book? Do some folding to find out.

1. Fold or roll pieces of paper into the shapes in the picture.
2. Try to balance a book on each shape. Now make up other shapes and try them, too.

Ready, set, go! Which piece of paper will win the Great Paper Race?

1. Find two sheets of paper that are exactly the same size.
2. Crumple one into a ball and leave the other flat.
3. Stand on a chair and drop the two pieces at the same time. Which one gets to the floor first? Race them again and see which one wins this time.

One, two, three... PULL!

PAPER CHALLENGE: TRY TO TEAR THIS PAPER INTO THREE.

Make two identical slits on the top of a piece of paper. Now hold the paper on each side and pull out to tear it. What happens?

Card Trick

**With a flick of your finger
you can drop a coin into a glass
without touching it.**

HERE'S HOW:

1. Place a playing card on top of a glass.

2. Put a coin on top of the card.

3. Quickly flick your index finger against the edge of the card. The card flies off, but what happens to the coin?

YOU CAN DROP A DIME INTO A SODA POP BOTTLE TOO.

Balance the coin on top of a strip of paper placed on top of an open bottle. Quickly pull the strip of paper out from under the dime.

What a way to save money!

Change

When you pop a piece of bread into your toaster, it comes out changed. It's crispy and warm instead of soft and cool. Lots of things change, including you. When you're born you need to be fed and cared for, but when you grow older you can feed and look after yourself. Batter changes into muffins if you add heat from an oven. Fruit can change from fresh to rotten over time. Sometimes you can even make something by putting two things together. Put a flame and some sticks together and you get a fire, which makes heat and light – perfect for roasting marshmallows.

You can change water into ice by putting it in the freezer. Take an ice cube from the freezer and put a wet piece of string on it. When you lift the string it sticks a little, but it comes off. Now sprinkle salt on your cube while the string is on top. Wait a few seconds and you should be able to lift the ice cube by lifting the string. Cool!

Bathtub Boats

Build a boat that will travel your tub.

1. Ask an adult to cut a medium milk carton in half lengthwise.

2. Staple a plastic straw on either side of the carton as shown in the diagram.

3. From the leftover carton, cut out a rectangle about two thumbs high and one thumb wide.

4. Slip a rubber band around the rectangle and staple securely in the middle on both sides.

5. Slip the rectangle's rubber band over the ends of the two straws. This makes a propeller.

6. Bend both ends of a third straw and slide them into the ends of the two side straws to form a frame for the propeller.

milk carton

Staple straws.

propeller

Staple rubber band.

rubber band

Slide straws together.

Launch Your Boat

Put your boat in water, wind up the rubber band, and away it goes!

Look at it go!

THE SPEEDBOAT

Cut a simple boat shape out of aluminum foil. Now dab a little liquid detergent on the back edge of the boat. Put the boat on soap-free water and step back for the takeoff!

Elec-tricks

Your hair will stand on end when you try this trick! It works best on a dry day and with squeaky clean hair.

HERE'S HOW:

1 Rub a blown-up balloon back and forth on your hair.

2 Look into a mirror and slowly pull the balloon away from your head.

3 Watch your hair rise!

4 Now hold the balloon against a wall. When you let it go, does it stick to the wall?

Can a comb pick up paper? Yes!...if it's full of static electricity.

1 Run a plastic comb through your hair several times.

2 Hold the comb near small pieces of tissue paper or bits of paper towel.

3 Watch the paper jump!

Watch the water wiggle!

YOU CAN MAKE WATER WIGGLE WITHOUT EVEN TOUCHING IT.

Turn on a cold water faucet and let the water flow in a slow, steady stream. Then run a plastic comb through your hair. Hold the comb beside the stream of water. What happens to the water when you move the comb back and forth?

Secret Messages

Send secret messages to a special friend!

HERE'S HOW:

1 Dip a toothpick or cotton swab in lemon juice and draw or print your message on plain paper.

2 Pour salt on the paper to completely cover the message.

3 When the paper is totally dry, brush away the salt.

4 To see the message, rub a pencil or crayon back and forth across the paper several times.

SUPER SECRET SAUCE

Mix two large spoonfuls of lemon juice with six spoonfuls of vegetable oil. If you let the mixture sit, the oil quickly floats to the top of the lemon juice. To make it stay together longer, add a spoonful or two of liquid honey. Mix it up well, then pour your sauce over some sliced fruit. Mmm!

This sauce is great on bananas!

Presto! Change-o!

Make dull pennies dazzle!

HERE'S HOW:

1. Fill a glass half full of vinegar.

2. Drop in old, tarnished pennies and stir.

3. Spoon out the shiny coins. How long do they stay bright?

TRY THE SAME EXPERIMENT AGAIN, BUT WITH A TWIST.

This time add a pinch or two of salt to the vinegar. Does the same thing happen? Then add a heaping spoonful of salt to the vinegar. What happens when these coins are left out to dry?

What a BRIGHT idea!

Egg Games

Did you know you can remove the shell of an egg without cracking it?

HERE'S HOW:

1. Carefully place an uncooked egg into a glass.

2. Add enough vinegar to cover the egg.

3. Wait for a day. Then gently lift the egg out of the glass. What does it feel like? What happens if you leave the egg covered in the vinegar for three or four days?

Have you ever tried to bounce an egg? Be sure to follow these steps before you do!

1. Place a hard-boiled egg in a glass.

2. Add enough vinegar to cover the egg.

3. After two days, how does the egg feel? Return the egg to the vinegar and wait one more day. Then gently bounce the egg. Try this in the kitchen sink first. How high can you bounce the egg?

That's really egg-citing!

HERE'S AN EGGS-TRA TRICK TO TRY: MAKE AN EGG FLOAT!

Place an uncooked egg in a glass of warm water and gently stir in a few spoonfuls of salt. Watch the egg rise.

Egg-citing Eggs

Make eggs bright and beautiful by adding a special ingredient.

HERE'S HOW:

1. Fill a small bowl with water and add ten drops of food coloring.

2. Place a hard-boiled egg in the water for about two minutes. Take the egg out and look at its color.

3. Now add three large spoonfuls of vinegar to the bowl.

4. Put the egg back in the bowl for two more minutes. Look at its color now. Wow! What a change.

TAKE A TWIRL TEST

Can you tell if an egg is hard-boiled or raw without cracking its shell? Just spin the egg on its side. A hard-boiled egg will spin much better than a raw one.

Hot and Cold

Can you make a balloon pop up without huffing and puffing?

HERE'S HOW:

1. Remove the cap from an empty pop bottle and put the bottle in a freezer for 15 minutes.

2. Blow up a small balloon to stretch it. Let the air out again.

3. Take the bottle out of the freezer, and pull the end of the balloon over the bottle opening.

4. Hold the bottle under your arm and watch the balloon pop up!

Wow! A bottle with a beat.

HAVE YOU EVER HEARD A BOTTLE TAPPING? FOLLOW THESE STEPS AND THEN LISTEN...

Put an empty pop bottle in the freezer for half an hour. Then take the bottle out and run water over the opening. Place a wet coin on top of the opening and cup your warm hands around the bottle. Now listen for the tap, tap, tap.

What Happened!

Fingerprints
(page 10)
Activity #1
False! No two people in the world, not even people from your family, have the exact same fingerprints. Identical twins don't have the same fingerprints. Did you know that no two cats have the same nose prints?

Activity #2
Loops are the most common finger print type.

Finger Power
(page 12)
Activity #1
When sitting, all your partner's weight is in his or her seat. To stand up, your partner's head must move forward to shift his weight to his legs. But, your finger stops your partner's head from moving. If your partner can't shift his weight to his legs, your partner can't stand up.

Activity #2
No, your partner can't hold his or her fists together so your fingers win every time. Your partner is pressing his or her fists together in an up-and-down direction. Your fingers hit the fists from the sides, the direction in which the muscles holding the fists together are the weakest.

Activity #3
You can't drop the penny. Your fingers move because there are tendons in your hands that attach your fingers to muscles. But, the tendons for your middle finger and your ring finger are joined together, so if your middle finger can't move, neither can your ring finger.

Taste Test
(page 14)
Activities #1 and #2
It's very hard to tell the apple slice from the potato slice. Your tongue can only tell you if food is sweet, sour, salty or bitter. You need your sense of smell to tell one food's flavor from another. If one slice was mushy and the other was hard you could tell them apart, but because they're both hard and crisp, you can't use that for a clue. For the same reasons it's also hard to tell the juices apart.

Color Vision
(page 16)
Activities #1 and #2
As the drop of water spreads out, it takes some of the black ink with it. Black ink is made up of many colors and you're seeing the different colors separate out of the spot of ink. The "heavy" colors stay near the center. "Light" ones spread out to the outside. In the same way, your murky mixture of colors separates out in the coffee filter.

Activity #3
As you blow into the water, the soap makes bubbles that spill over the glass and onto the paper. The soap carries some of the water and food coloring with it onto the paper. Wow, a bubble pattern!

Eye Openers
(page 18)
Activity #1
These are all optical illusions — things that trick your eyes and fool your brain. In Trick #1 you see vases if you notice the color, or faces if you notice the white space around the color. In Trick #2, all the flower centers are the same size but they look different because you use the sizes of the other circles to judge the size of the middle circle. In Trick #3, can you see the duck or the rabbit? If you stare at Trick #4 long enough, you should see grey circles appear and disappear between the squares. And, both stars in Trick #5 are the

same color, but your eyes might think they're different because of the colors they're beside.

Activity #2
You see a floating finger because your eyes are not looking right at your fingertips. When you look past your fingers, each eye is looking at your fingertips from a different angle and so each eye sends your brain a slightly different message. Your brain gets an overlapping image of both fingertips and that's what makes the floating finger.

Hole in Your Hand
(page 20)
Activity #1
You use both your eyes to see things. Your brain receives a message from each eye and puts them together to make the total picture. In this trick, one eye sees your hand and the other sees the opening through the tube. When these two pictures are put together in your brain, you think you see a hole in your hand.

Body Tricks
(page 22)
Activity #1
To hop forward in that position, you have to be able to shift your weight forward, but you can't so you fall over. You can keep your balance to "shuffle hop" backwards, but you can't get off the ground because you can't move your knees. The muscles in your feet and ankles aren't strong enough to lift your body off the ground.

Activity #2
Eyesight is one of the senses that affects your balance. Standing on one leg unbalances you until you move your body to get your balance back again. If you can't see, your brain can't get enough information to tell your body how to move to keep you balanced.

Activity #3
Surprise! Your foot and forearm are exactly the same size! This is true for people of all ages.

Plant Power
(page 26)
Activity #1
Beans, like all other green plants, need water and light to make food and to grow. Plants grow in the direction of the most light. The only light in the box is through the hole at the end, so the beans grow in that direction instead of straight up.

Activity #2
Seeds take in water, swell, and break open as they grow. As your beans take in water, they press harder and harder on the sides of the glass as they swell. Finally, the plastic glass can't take the pressure and it cracks.

Plant Fun
(page 28)
Activity #1
All plants need water, and all plants have tiny tubes inside their stems to carry water from their roots to their leaves. The colored water lets you see that water has moved from the glass, up through the celery stem, to the celery leaves. If you cut the celery's stem in half you can see the tubes because they're colored too.

Activity #2
The carrots we eat are really big roots. They move food and water from the ground and pass it onto the green leaves so the carrot plant can grow. There's just enough food left in the carrot top for the leaves to sprout. The leaves will grow for a few days, but when the food is all used up, they'll wilt.

Night Lights
(page 30)

Activity #1

The moon fits in the hole both times. Some scientists think that the moon seems to change size because you can compare it with trees and buildings when it has just risen. When it is high in the sky it just seems smaller because there is nothing large to compare it with.

Activity #2

Even on a hot day, there are always tiny bits of water, called moisture, in the air. The cold water and ice in the glass cools the air that's next to it. When air cools, it can't hold as much water so the water comes out of the air and settles onto the sides of the glass. That's why there is dew on the grass after a cool night — the air got cooler so the water had to settle out of the air and onto the ground.

Water Power
(page 32)

Activity #1

When you tip the jar, you make waves. The water hits the end of the jar and bounces back to the other end of the jar. It's easy to see the waves because water and oil slosh back and forth without mixing. Also, the oil slows down the water wave because the water has to push the oil out of the way. When the water pushes some of the oil out of the way, the rest of the oil goes with it so you see nice rolling waves.

Activity #2

The cone closed up! When you put the pinecone in water, it takes in water and swells up. The swelling makes the pinecone's scales bend up and close. When pinecones first grow on pine trees, they're moist and closed up tight. As they dry out, the scales open and the tree's seeds fall out. Let your pinecone dry out and it will open up again.

Spin Away
(page 34)

Activity #1

When you swirl the jar, all the water inside travels quickly around the jar in a circle leaving a hollow space in the middle. The swirling motion also makes bubbles from the soap you added. The swirling water pulls all the bubbles to the center of the jar and you see a tornado. Real tornados are made of swirling wind.

Activity #2

When you shake the jar, the marbles move around inside and stir up the cream. All the mixing makes heat that lets the bits of fat in the cream stick together. When the fat sticks together, it makes a soft butter. The liquid that's left behind is watery milk.

Bubble, Bubble
(page 36)

Activities #1 and #2

Some of the bubbles in the soda water collect on the raisins. The bubbles rise to the top carrying the raisins with them. When the bubbles reach the top and burst, the raisins sink again. The bubbles also lift the spaghetti pieces, but because they are lighter they rise more easily. The bubbles are made of a gas called carbon dioxide — the same gas you breathe out.

Activity #3

Raisins were once fat juicy grapes that were picked and dried in the sun. When your raisins fill up with water or soda water, they go back to their first grape shape!

Water Surprises

(page 40)

Activities #1 and #2

Water is clear, but when you look through it, it changes the way you see things. In Activity #1 looking through the water flips the arrow so that it looks backward to you. In Activity #2 the straw appears to separate or disappear as you move it around because you are looking through the water. Pour the water out and the straw stays straight and you can see it all the time.

Lost and Found

(page 42)

Activities #1 and #2

When you look through the water at an angle you can't see the coin. If you pour the water out and look through the glass at the same angle you can see the coin. Water changes the way you see things. In a similar way, when you look through the water at an angle, the pencil seems to be broken, but if you pour the water out it looks whole again.

Bag Boggle

(page 44)

Activity #1

When you pierce the plastic bag, the plastic pulls together around the pencil to seal up the hole. Then no water can escape. Plastic bags are made to be strong and stretchy.

Activity #2

When you press the plastic bag against the inside of the glass, you push out the air. There is less air between the bag and the glass than there is above and outside the glass. The air above and outside the glass presses the bag to the glass so you can barely budge the bag. If you put a tiny hole in the bag, air rushes in underneath and out comes the bag.

High and Dry

(page 46)

Activity #1

When you turn the glass upside down, air gets trapped inside the glass. The trapped air pushes against the water when you put the glass in the water. The air keeps the water out of the glass and the paper stays dry.

Activity #2

It is impossible to fold any piece of paper in half more than nine times!

Heart to Heart

(page 48)

Activity #1

When you blow between the hearts, you make fast-moving air. This moving air doesn't press out on the hearts as hard as non-moving air. That lets the non-moving air outside the hearts push in on the hearts, making them touch.

Activity #2

The card spins so fast that your eye still holds a picture of the first side when the second side appears. You end up seeing both sides together. Did you know that this is the same way you see a movie? Movies are made of lots of still pictures that flash by your eyes quickly. Instead of seeing lots of still pictures, you see movement.

Up and Away!

(page 50)

Activity #1

When you throw the plane, the round shape of each loop moves air more quickly over the top of the plane than under the plane. The faster the air moves the less it presses on the plane. So, the plane gets a stronger push from below than from above which keeps it in the air. As long as the plane moves quickly through the air, it will fly. When it slows down, it falls to the ground.

Activity #2

When you blow into the thin straw, air hits the tape that covers the end of the big straw and pushes the big straw off the thin straw. The air then carries the big straw through the air for a little bit.

Paper Power

(page 52)

Activity #1

The accordion shape and the tube hold up the book the best. The open book shape and the tent shape fall down under the heavy book because one part of the paper shape is weaker than another part. Which shape is best? Press down on all the shapes and you'll find that the tube is the strongest. This shape is often used in construction because it is so strong.

Activity #2

The flat piece of paper has much more surface for air to go around as it falls towards the ground. This slows down the flat paper and the crumpled piece wins every time.

Activity #3

Why does the paper always rip into only two pieces? As you pull the paper sideways, your pull is never exactly the same on both sides. One is weaker and one is stronger. And, your two cuts are never exactly the same although they look the same. For these two reasons, your paper will tear at either one cut or the other.

Card Trick

(page 54)

Activities #1 and #2

When you flick the card, it moves so quickly that it flies right out from under the coin and the coin drops into the glass. The card is smooth and shiny so it easily slips out from under the coin without making the coin move. In much the same way, the dime drops into the soda bottle when you quickly pull the strip of paper away.

Bathtub Boats

(page 58)

Activity #1

When you wind up the rubber band, energy is stored in the band. When you let go, the band unwinds changing that stored energy to movement. The unwinding band turns the propeller and pushes the boat through the water.

Activity #2

Water behaves like it has a clear elastic skin on its surface. As soon as you add the soap you change the water's skin. The soap from the boat breaks the skin so it pulls back toward the sides of the basin, taking the boat with it.

Elec-tricks

(page 60)

Activities #1, #2, and #3

When you rub the balloon on your hair you make static electricity. The balloon can then stick to the wall and make your hair stand up. The comb picks up static electricity from your hair the same way. That's why it attracts the pieces of tissue paper or paper towel to make them jump. And that's why it attracts the water making it wiggle.

Secret Messages

(page 62)

Activity #1

When you put the salt on the lemon juice, some of the salt mixes with the juice and then dries onto the paper. That means that when you brush away the salt, you leave behind small salt crystals with sharp edges on your message. Then, as you rub the pencil over the paper, more lead catches on the salt crystals than on the rest of the paper. That's why your secret message appears.

Activity #2

Oil and lemon juice don't mix well, but when you add honey it changes things. Honey makes the oil break into tiny drops that will mix evenly through the lemon juice. The sauce will stay mixed for a while, but it will separate if it sits long enough.

Presto! Change-o!
(page 64)
Activities #1 and #2

Over time pennies get dirty. Vinegar is an acid that eats away the dirt to change the dirty pennies to clean and shiny pennies. Salt mixes with the vinegar to make a stronger acid that works even faster. When the pennies cleaned with salt and vinegar are left out in the air, they change again by turning green. If you don't want your pennies to turn green, wash them with detergent as soon as you take them out of the salt and vinegar mixture, then rinse and dry them.

Egg Games
(page 66)
Activities #1 and #2

Eggshells contain a hard material called calcium, the same stuff in your bones and teeth. Calcium helps make them strong. Vinegar is an acid which dissolves the calcium in the shell leaving the skin under the shell to hold the egg together. In the same way vinegar attacks the eggshell, acids in your mouth can attack your teeth and make holes in them. That's why brushing your teeth is so important.

Activity #3

At first the egg sinks because it is heavier than water. When you add salt, you change the freshwater to saltwater. The saltwater is heavier than the egg so the egg floats. That's why it's easier for you to float in saltwater like an ocean than it is to float in a freshwater lake or swimming pool.

Egg-citing Eggs
(page 68)
Activity #1

An eggshell is smooth and hard so food coloring can't stick to the shell very well. Vinegar is an acid that changes the eggshell. It eats away at the outside of the shell making it rough and porous. Now more of the food coloring can soak into the shell.

Activity #2

When you spin a raw egg, the liquid inside moves around, slowing the egg down. The hardboiled egg spins faster and better because its insides have been changed to a solid. The solid insides don't move around so they don't slow the egg down.

Hot and Cold
(page 70)
Activities #1 and #2

Cold air takes up less room than hot air. When you change the air temperature by heating up the cold air in the bottle with your body heat, the warmed air expands and takes up more space. In Activity #1 this expanding air has nowhere to go but into the balloon. The warmed air in Activity #2 escapes out the top of the bottle a little at a time, lifting the coin up and dropping it.

Science Concepts

ooking for an experiment that explores a specific scientific principle? The list below shows where to find the activities in the book that introduce some important scientific concepts. Because they are quite abstract, most of these concepts are not dealt with by name in the experiments or in the notes under *What Happened!* But the list is useful for adults or older children to connect the understanding that comes by seeing and doing the experiments with a broader view of scientific principles.

Absorption
Bubble, Bubble challenge, 37
Plant Power, 27
Water Power challenge, 32

Acid
Egg Games, 66
Egg-citing Eggs, 68
Presto! Change-o!, 64

Air Pressure
Bag Boggle challenge, 44
Heart to Heart, 48

Bernoulli's Principle
Heart to Heart, 48

Capillary Action
Color Vision, 17
Plant Fun, 28

Center of Gravity
Body Tricks, 22

Condensation
Night Lights challenge, 30

Crystals
Secret Messages, 63

Density
Egg Games challenge, 66

Emulsion
Secret Messages challenge, 63

Evaporation
Night Lights challenge, 30
Secret Messages, 63

Flight
Up and Away!, 51

Flotation
Bathtub Boats, 59
Bubble, Bubble, 37
Egg Games challenge, 66

Friction
Card Trick, 55

Inertia
Card Trick, 55

Kinetic Energy
Bathtub Boats, 59

Lens
Water Surprises, 41

Lift
Up and Away!, 51

Newton's First Law of Motion
Card Trick, 55

Optical Illusions
Eye Openers, 18-19

Oxidation
Presto! Change-o!, 64

Persistence of Vision
Heart to Heart challenge, 48

Phototrophism
Plant Power, 26

Polyethylene Plastic
Bag Boggle, 44

Potential Energy
Bathtub Boats, 59

Refraction of Light
Lost and Found, 43
Water Surprises, 41

Static Electricity
Elec-tricks, 61

Surface Tension
Bathtub Boats challenge, 59

Thermal Conduction
Hot and Cold, 70

Vortex
Spin Away!, 34

Wave Motion
Water Power, 32

Index

A

air, expanding 70
air pressure 44, 46, 48

B

balance 22
balloon 60, 70
beans 26
boats 59
bubbles 17, 34, 37
butter 34

C

card 55
carrot 28
celery 28
coins 12, 20, 43, 55, 64
comb 60
color 17, 19, 28

D

detergent 17, 34, 59
dew 30
dissolving eggshell 66, 68

E

eggs 66, 68
eyesight 18-19, 20, 22, 41, 48

F

finger, floating 18
fingerprints 10
fingers, strength of 12
flight 51
floating
    boats 59
    egg 66
    finger 18
    raisins 37
    spaghetti 37
forearm, size 22
foot, size 22
fruit juice 63
fruit sauce 63

G

glider 51

H

honey 63

I

ice 30
ink, black 17

L

lemon juice 63

M

moon 30

O

oil, vegetable 32, 63

P

paper 30, 52
pencil 43, 44, 63
pennies, cleaning 64
pinecone 32
plane 51
plants 26

S

salt 63, 64, 66
sandwich bag 44
smell, sense of 15
sprouting 28
static electricity 60
straws 51, 59
structural strength 52

T

taste, sense of 15
tornado 34

V

vinegar 64, 66, 68

W

water 27, 28, 30, 32, 34,
.................41, 43, 44, 46, 59, 60
waves 32
whip cream 34